Polymorphism:

As It Is Played

Joseph Bergin, Ph.D.

Polymorphism:
As It Is Played

Joseph Bergin, Ph. D.

Published by Slant Flying Press, 2015

ISBN 978-1-940113-05-0

Caveat: While the people named in this work are real, living, vibrant human beings, all code and conversations come from the imagination of the author. The errors, of course, are my own.

Cover: Great Peng Mounts the Sky. Great Peng is a mythical Chinese monster that is both fish and bird. The cover image represents Peng in its bird aspect. It is *Wing of the Peng*, from the Kyōka Hyaku Monogatari manuscript of 1852.

Printed: July 15, 2015

Introduction

This little book weaves together a few themes that should be known by every programmer that uses an Object-Oriented language such as Java or Python. The main theme is *Polymorphism*, which gives the programmer a clean way to program alternative actions in a program. The big idea is that a fragment of code should do exactly one thing in a simple way.

A second theme is building applications using *Piecemeal Growth*, rather than overall implementation of a predefined design. A program grows organically, and the needs of users may change, even over the course of development. This means that the program built is what its sponsor wanted at the end of development, which may be different from the perceived needs at the start.

We also show how to use two important tools, Eclipse and JUnit, to implement a program using *Test Driven Development*. This simple idea is profound. The programmer writes tests immediately before the code that is being tested. The names of program actions used in the tests then become the names of methods in the application. So, a certain low level of design is done in the test framework. An implication of this is that the first time the programmer sees and uses a name it is in an applied use, not its definition. Thus, you get a sense of what it will be like in use.

The vehicle for all of this is a hypothetical set of conversations between two students building a project for a professor. The students discuss their issues and decisions as they go along and develop the program one *Story* at a time. Each story introduces one desired feature of the result. In this project, the professor has sequenced the stories to relieve the students of problems of design.

This case study is not about building large things from independent parts. It gives a different view of Object-Orientation. *Suppose that you have to build a single class that exhibits complex behavior*. You want the code to be as simple as possible. But even if you are building a large program, you still need to build the individual classes. Perhaps like this...

Acknowledgements

OpenClipArt.org for the images used here, other than the cover

  Gubrww2

  Kevie: http://www.kevie.co.uk

  Liftarn: www.interface1.net.webloc

  Merlin2525: http://merlin2525.deviantart.com/

  Ouisa: http://www.ousia.tk

  Studio_Hades: http://www.acheron-mint.com

I thank the following readers who gave valuable feedback on the project. First, Julie Gill and Zahid Mahir, whose imagined conversations you will read here. Other readers are Lisa Bergin, Rinaldo DiGiorgio, Christian Köppe, Richard Pattis, and James Roberts. Christian provided the UML diagram near the end of the book. Barbara Esmark gave early advice on layouts.

Thanks, also, to Ward Cunningham for hosting some of my work, referenced here, at **http://fed.wiki.org**.

This book is dedicated to the thousands of students I've been proud to teach over the years. I hope your lives and careers continue to go well.

Additional information about this book can be found at
  http://csis.pace.edu/~bergin/polymorphismBook

> Hints and comments to the reader will appear as we go along in a box like this one. Some things are explained in the **Notes** section near the end of the book. Web searches will also be a fruitful source of information about a few things mentioned in passing.
>
> The author assumes that the reader can write a simple Java class, create objects, and has an understanding of simple statements, reference variables, and messages to objects.

Contents

Inspiration

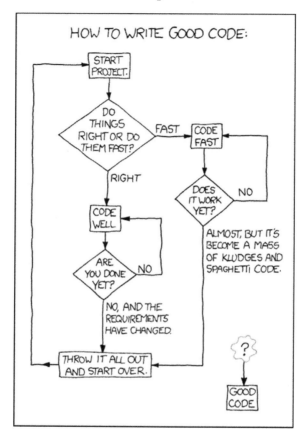

http://xkcd.com/844

Begin At The Beginning

So, you are a student learning to program in a language like Java. You have a lot of things to learn. Among them, is how to approach a problem and structure your efforts, as well as using the language effectively. We'll assume you have learned a few things about Java already.

This book will weave together a number of related themes, the most important of which is *Polymorphism*, the essence of Object-Oriented Programming. Polymorphism is a way to structure your program so that things fit together smoothly without the ad hoc decision making that requires IF statements.

The focus will be on building a single important class, perhaps as part of a larger whole. The class will exhibit complexity, but it is good to control that complexity: to keep it simple.

You should try to imagine the program as an interlocking set of very simple parts. The parts are simple to imagine, write, test, and use. The complexity of the program is in the interactions between the parts, not the parts themselves. The parts, actually objects, are built, and their classes written, only when we know we need them.

Additionally, we will introduce a few of the practices that come from *Extreme Programming*, a flavor of *Agile Software Development*. In particular we will show Pair Programming, Test First Development, and problem specification by *Stories* rather than via a complete technical description of the desired result. The programmers, here students, always work in pairs, shoulder to shoulder, on one simple story at a time, first writing a few tests so that they can be assured that when they code the application itself they "get it right" and that they don't break the program later when adding other parts.

In this book we will follow two students, Julie and Zahid, who know a fair amount about programming but want to delve deeper. The project assigned by their professor, Professor Bergin (aka Dr. J), is to build a simple, four function integer-valued calculator. Perhaps...?

1

No, no, no.

NO!

Much too complex. More like this…

Ah, yes. Much better.

In fact, we won't bother with the above human-centered interface at all, but simply build the underlying functionality that would support this kind of physical design. So don't take the above image too literally. It is only a kind of *metaphor* for what is wanted.

The underlying architecture we are assuming here is called Model-View-Controller (MVC). The above image is a possible *View* of the application. The connection between the buttons and the functionality is the *Controller*. But we shall build the *Model*: the logic of the application itself. Many applications that have a Graphical User Interface (GUI), such as this one, use some variation of MVC as an architecture, or basic structure.

Let's meet some of the players. The most important are the two students, Julie and Zahid. Both are in their second year of study and both are smart and hard working. Julie was born in the south-western part of the United States, and Zahid in Afghanistan. Your author was proud to teach students like these.

Here is Julie:

And, this is Zahid:

We shall see a lot of them.

Julie and Zahid have been given an assignment by Dr. J. They meet in some *real-world* space, perhaps a lab, in which they can work together at the same computer. One of them at a time will be programming and the other looking on and commenting, making suggestions. The keyboard will pass back and forth every few minutes. This is called *Pair Programming*. The person with the keyboard is called the *driver* and the other is the *navigator*. Both roles are essential. Pairing in virtual space is possible, but harder.

Pair Programming is used in many industrial settings and is useful for those learning to program as well. One key idea in pair programming is that it is harder to get stuck. Two heads are better than one, and each person can aid the development of the other.

In fact, in practice, it turns out that the driver tends to look at the code he or she is writing very tactically: a small scale, microscopic, view. The navigator, on the other hand, naturally thinks more strategically, not having the responsibility of getting the details correct at that moment. Synergy. Copacetic.

If the project were a bit bigger there might be a larger team, but all programming done in pairs. Paring would rotate through the team. Over the course of the term, team members will get experience working with several people, sharing their talents. This, itself, is a necessary skill for a career in computing, as it is in most fields.

There are some intellectual tasks that should be done alone, but programming is not one of them.

The space in which they meet could as well be a coffee shop. Discos don't work as well, however. Programming and *raving* have never been especially compatible, even when discos actually existed.

When Dr J. gave the assignment he discussed it in class for a while. The students asked questions about it and the professor answered, though not always completely. The students have a general, but somewhat indistinct view of what must be built. It is mostly about scope and vision, not detail. Dr. J will expect more questions as the project progresses. He gets a lot of email, of course.

Julie and Zahid are about to start. Let's listen in...

Zahid: Hi Julie.

Hi Zahid. I guess we need to work together on the calculator program. Have you done one of these before.

Nope. Shouldn't be too bad. Here are the stories. Twelve of them.

A Story is a short description of a program feature, written on a card. The twelve stories can be found starting on page 83.

Shall we just split them up and do it? Six each?

Wellll....

6

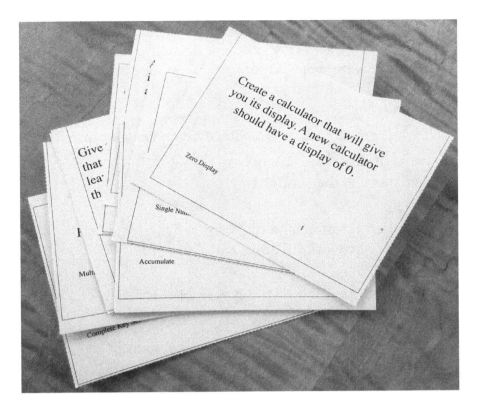

A simple application such as this has only a few stories. But a commercial product can have hundreds of stories. They are written over time, not necessarily at the start of development. They may change as needs change. Stories may be dropped or added at well defined check points. But the set of stories to be worked on over a couple of weeks (an *iteration*) is small, fixed, and stable.

A story doesn't completely specify a feature, so the person who wrote the story needs to remain available to give clarifications. He or she is also the final judge of when the story's development is complete. Here the professor fulfills this role, called the *customer*.

Story cards are *named* (for communication) and *numbered* (so that they are less likely to get misplaced). But they aren't necessarily completed in numeric order. It is up to the customer to group them and the programmers to decide on order of development for that group. Here a group will consist of just one card.

Back to our programmers...

Julie: Actually, Dr. J said to work story by story using Test Driven Development. Working together on each story.

Test Driven Development?

Right. We write tests for a story before we write the code to implement it.

See, we use JUnit* to manage the tests and we only work 'til tests pass.

Never tried it. Work?

Yeah. It's kind of cool. Geeky tho'.

That's us, for sure.

Yeah.

And we never work independently, dividing the work?

Right again.

OK, I'm game.

Kent Beck, the creator of Extreme Programming (XP), and Joe Bergin, Dr. J, meet somewhere in cyberspace...

Kent   **Joe**

So, I hear you use Story Driven Development in teaching.

> Yep. Students initially have a hard time breaking a problem down into parts. So I just give them the parts. They never see a full narrative form of the requirements.

And you sequence them too?

> Yes. Just about as if I were their customer in an XP project, but with one story per iteration. The first few stories are easy and then it builds up.

Do they estimate time for the stories and the whole thing?

> No, not at the beginning. Though I ask them to record the actual time. I'm not teaching XP, just programming. Many of the XP practices help. Pairing, Testing...

So they don't need to do high level design.

> Right. They just build small parts and make them fit together. But my real goal is teaching Polymorphism within this framework.

Let's go back to the students, who are starting work.

> Create a calculator that will give you its display. A new calculator should have a display of 0.
>
> Zero Display   1

Zahid: Well, what does the first story say?

Julie: Just, "When you turn a calculator on, its display should be 0."

Well, what should it look like? This?

It doesn't look like anything. We are just building the program logic, not the views. It just needs to have a useful set of methods.

Oh. OK.

Ron Jeffries, creator of JUnit, and Dr. J meet in cyberspace.

Ron	Joe
Kent tells me you use Test Driven Development and JUnit in the classroom.	
	Right. It is hard to convince students that testing speeds them up and reduces frustration, tho.
All newcomers have that problem. It doesn't take too long to get into the swing.	
	Tools like Eclipse* that help them manage the files are a big help too. And Eclipse makes the test runs simple. A few examples done in class get them going.
Your stories are pretty simple. That must help at the start.	
	Better, it is great when any errors show up immediately so they can be fixed before your mind wanders on to other issues.
Nothing worse than wasting time figuring out why it doesn't work. True even for pros. Especially for pros.	
	Amen, brother.
Who writes the tests?	
	I do some of them and they do others. I stay available to help as needed. I'm their customer.

Julie (typing)   Zahid (watching)

The first test is pretty simple.

```
package juliezahid.calculator;
import static org.junit.Assert.*;
import org.junit.Before;
import org.junit.Test;

public class CalculatorModelTest {
```

So here is the first test. I'll need
some names for things. Hmmm...

12

```
package juliezahid.calculator;
import static org.junit.Assert.*;
import org.junit.Before;
import org.junit.Test;

public class CalculatorModelTest {

    private CalculatorModel model = new CalculatorModel();

    @Test
    public void test() {
        assertEquals(0, model.display());
    }
}
```

Zahid: Test? Assert? Model?

Julie: Well, I created a new CalculatorModel named *model* and wrote a test for its display. I'm asserting it's initially zero. The words Test and assertEquals are JUnit magic, I guess.

But we don't have code for any of that? CalculatorModel?

That's why it's called Test *FIRST*. JUnit *does* stuff. The asserts are built in. I made up the names CalculatorModel and display.

Dr. J wanders past and looks over their shoulders at the screen. Without commenting he notes the following, with approval.

Julie has named the package for both of them and the project itself.

She has decided here, within the test framework, that they will later create a class named *CalculatorModel* for the application itself.

Likewise she has named this test class appropriately.

Julie has also decided that the CalculatorModel class will have a method named *display* that will return the display value as an integer. This is actually a very low level of program design.

However, her test method seems poorly named: *test*. It might better be *testInitialZero*. The names of tests usually begin "test...".

All seems well for a start.

• • •

Note, that no code for the application has been written and the CalculatorModel class doesn't yet exist. This test will fail. It won't even compile. But since they are using Eclipse, a button click will cause the framework to create a the class, and another will create the *display* method skeleton within it, which they can edit.

The first few lines shown here are standard boilerplate. The annotation @Test tells the test framework that the next method is a test to be automatically executed on any test run. Some versions of JUnit required the tests be named test..., but @Test flags the test methods.

• • •

Dr. J passes on, deep in thought: "I'd better give them a list of background readings. Maybe an Eclipse tutorial..."

Julie still has the keyboard, but it is also common practice to switch at this point and have Zahid build enough to make this test pass. He would then write another, failing, test for this or the next story and Julie would make that test pass, etc. Let's see what they do...

Zahid: So we claim in this test that if we create a model object and ask for its display we get zero.

Exactly.

Now we need to write the *CalculatorModel* class and give it a *display* method, just like we promise in this test.

OK. Let me take over as driver.

OK, I'll navigate.

There are lots of errors indicated here, I see. Missing parts.

Right. The errors are underlined.

Driver: The person in control of the keyboard and mouse.

Navigator: The person who watches and advises.

Zahid: You said Eclipse will help me create the skeletons for the missing pieces? It'll make a new file and everything?

Right. Just hover the mouse over an underlined error.

Here we go. (Hovers, selects "create class..." from the menu and fills in the resulting dialog. Similar steps for the display method.)

```
package juliezahid.calculator;
public class CalculatorModel {
    public Object display() {
            // TODO Auto-generated method stub
            return null;
    }
}
```

Cool.

Very cool. We have our class and method stub. So, now we can fix it up to pass the test. It should return an int of zero instead of the null object value, I think.

Right. (does it)

16

```
package juliezahid.calculator;
public class CalculatorModel {
    public int display() {
            return 0;
    }
}
```

Now to run the test file as a *JUnit test*, right.

Yep. Look. A green bar. It passes.
We expected 0 and got 0.

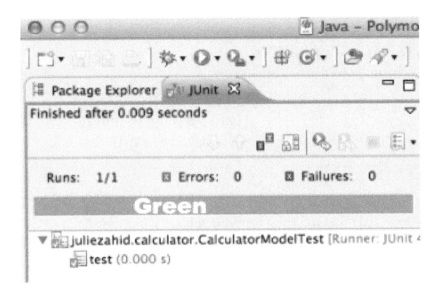

Are we done with the story?

Only when we can't think of any thing else that could go wrong. I can't. You?

Nope. Cool. One story done. Maybe it would be better to give the test a better name, though. Just *test* is a bit too generic. How is the design?

OK for now, I think. Simple anyway. I'll leave the test for now. We can always change it later. And test names aren't referenced from elsewhere anyway.

Oh, we are also supposed to record how long it took to build each Story.

That was only 20 minutes. Shall I write it on the card?

Do It.

They have code that returns 0 for the display of a new calculator and they have a test to verify it. That is all the story called for.

Dr J: Programmers have been conditioned to write general, rather than specific, code. You were probably taught that it would be better above to create a field with a value of zero and return that from the *display* method instead. That would be OK, but in doing that you are anticipating some further use that isn't implicit in the story being developed. Julie and Zahid were correct to return the constant 0 from the method, since that is all that was mentioned.

In Extreme Programming, we call this "doing the simplest thing that could possibly work." The reason that the more general code is normally preferred is that the programmer usually works from a more complete specification, rather than a simple story. In XP, we don't anticipate future stories since they might change or be dropped. Dr. J might suddenly change the assignment into a Coffee Machine instead of a Calculator after only one story.

We don't assume here that we will touch a piece of code only once, but, rather, are happy to return to it if a future failing test makes it necessary. If the IDE (Integrated Development Environment) is powerful enough, as Eclipse is, the failing test will point you to the place that failed. Other IDEs, such as NetBeans can also do this.

Note that when we run tests, we automatically run them all, not just the most recent. Then, if a new story requires a change in things, a test will fail and we can fix the application. But we don't spend time and effort on building things we might not need. Change happens. Anticipate it. Embrace it.

Of course the question arises as to whether the programmers have enough tests, or even the correct tests. Note for now that if the programmers themselves write the tests they are testing only their own *understanding* of the requirements. Dr. J may have a different understanding. We will return to this issue later.

Note how simple the test was. Too simple? Its value is not in getting the story right the first time. Most decent programmers can do that. The real value is in assuring that you don't break code you wrote earlier while adding new code. Old tests will immediately fail if you go wrong, alerting you to the problem. That is a Big Idea.

Professor **Laurie Williams** of NCSU and Dr. J have a chat at an academic conference:

Joe	Laurie
Pair Programming is really working well in my intro programming classes. Thanks for all your work on that.	
	Yep, pairing is great. The synergy between students is really powerful. Two working together can make more progress since they aren't as likely to get stuck at the same place.
Right. So when one gets stuck the other can move the pair forward.	
	Yes, and they can help each other learn It also fosters cooperation, which they will need later in their work – and careers.
Intellectual integrity means something different in this world. Also ownership.	
	The pair, or more generally, the team, owns the product collectively. They share the rewards, too.
And switching the pairs around during the course gives them experience working with a variety of folks.	
	Right. Many, many advantages.

In The Groove

After a break, Zahid and Julie meet again in the lab.

Hi Julie. Let's try this. I'll write a test. You make it pass, and then you create a new test that I'll make pass.

So we pass driving back and forth at each test. Sounds good. Go for it.

That is a good development plan for a pair.

OK, the *Single Numeric Key* story talks about number keys. I'll write a test for the 3 key.

Give the calculator keys like 3 and 5. When you press a single key the value should show in the display.

Single Numeric Key   2

Zahid types...

OK. The test just asserts that if we tell the model *pressThree*, then the display is 3.

You just decided that the CalculatorModel should have a *pressThree* method. Isn't that design?

Pretty low level, but yeah. I'm driving, remember?

Right. I guess that's OK, but why not parametrize it with something like press(3)?

But then you could say press(42). No calculator has such a key.

Not in this universe, anyway.

The navigator is making suggestions for alternatives as they occur to her. The driver can accept them or not, usually after a bit of discussion. The navigator is an *active* observer. The driver maintains control.

```
@Test
public void testSingle3Key() {
        model.pressThree();
        assertEquals(3, model.display());
}
```

This is what the complete test file looks like now:

```
package juliezahid.calculator;

import static org.junit.Assert.*;
import org.junit.Before;
import org.junit.Test;

public class CalculatorModelTest {

    private CalculatorModel model = new CalculatorModel();

    @Test
    public void test() {
            assertEquals(0, model.display());
    }

    @Test
    public void testSingle3Key() {
            model.pressThree();
            assertEquals(3, model.display());
    }

}
```

Note that there are now two tests in the same file. Work will need to be done in the application itself to make them both pass. The test for the 5 key will be just like the one for the 3 key.

JUnit will automatically run each of the test methods separately, just after initializing a new *model* variable. In other words, with two methods, there will be two model objects created, one for each test method and two independent test *runs*. Each test method will refer to a distinct model object. Tests are independent of each other. JUnit has quite a few more capabilities than are shown here, of course.

Julie: OK, back to me. It doesn't even compile yet. It fails until we have a *pressThree* method in the model class. Easy enough to get the skeleton, but then what. It still fails, of course.

```java
public void pressThree() {
        // TODO Auto-generated method stub
}
```

The display method will still return 0.

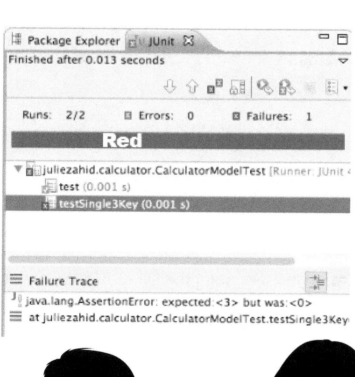

I guess we need a *display* field in the class. Initially 0.

Right. Then *pressThree* could set it to 3. And, and, and

and the *display* method returns the value of the *display* field. Like this....

How about the tests?

Green bar. Test passes. Actually both tests pass. Now I'll write a similar test for the five key and you make it pass. (Types)

OK. Not very interesting though. (Types) All the other keys would be the same. Let's end with the five key for now and move on. Only 15 minutes for that.

I've got half an hour before I need to go pick up my mom.

OK, let's do another story.

Hopefully something more challenging.

Be careful what you wish for.

So this is the state of the model itself. Of course the test for the five key was also added to the test class.

```
package juliezahid.calculator;

/** A model for a four function integer valued calculator. The
 * calculator uses algebraic (not RPN) logic.
 * @author julie and zahid
 */
public class CalculatorModel {

    private int display = 0;

    /** Retrieve the current display value of the calculator
     * @return the current display of the calculator
     */
    public int display() {
        return display;
    }

    /** The three key on the calculator is pressed.
     */
    public void pressThree() {
        this.display = 3;
    }

    /** The five key on the calculator is pressed.
     */
    public void pressFive() {
        this.display = 5;
    }

}
```

Note that only four lines (other than comments) were actually typed by the programmers. The rest was inserted by Eclipse.

Also, the *display* method has a new version here.

Zahid: OK, What's next? I think we can call Story 2 done, though we'll need to come back and put in the other keys.

The next one is about multiple key presses. When you press five then three, you get fifty-three in the display. [See pg. 83]

The logic is to multiply the display by 10 and then add in the new key. But write the test so I can make it pass.

Sure. (types)

```
@Test
public void testMultipleKeys(){
    model.pressFive();
    model.pressThree();
    assertEquals(53, model.display());
}
```

Done – and a red bar. The display should be 53 but is 3, the last key pressed.

My turn. Where shall we put the code? I guess we can put it in the press methods, like this. (types)

```
public void pressFive(){
   display = display * 10 + 5;
}
```

But then you need to repeat almost the same code for all ten keys. Parametrize it, I think. Private helper method.

Right. Of course. Needs a parameter so we can fire it from each press method. (types into CalculatorModel class) And the press methods look like this.

```
private void accumulate(int n){
    display = display * 10 + n;
}
public void pressFive(){
    accumulate(5)
}
```

Now the test...Bingo. Green. Another card, another story, another success. Love it.

But wouldn't *keyValue* be a better name than *n* for the parameter? Clearer.

Why not. Easy to do. (types)

Dr. J has wandered through the lab again, trolling for questions. After a while he goes to his office and thinks a bit about *refactoring*.

• • •

Refactoring is changing the structure of some code without altering its function. The intent is to improve it for the future, either to make it more understandable or to make later changes easier. It is how you improve the architecture, or structure, of the code a bit at a time rather than having to commit to an overall structure at the start.

The first refactoring was to take the version in which the formula for the accumulation was repeated in each press method and make a helper method. The original idea violates the *Say It Once* principle. This sort of refactoring is very common. Eclipse provides direct support for this and other simple cases.

Then, Julie did a very minor additional refactoring by renaming a parameter to make it more *intention revealing*. The name *n* was very generic, but the intended use of the helper method is to accumulate a key value. Note that the code worked fine before this change. It passed the tests. After the change it still does, so the functionality hasn't changed.

An alternate design here would be to create a helper object (and associated class) to hold the *accumulate* method, but that would be over-kill. The programmers did the simplest reasonable thing. The object they might have built would have given no advantage over the simple method.

• • •

Dr. J reminds himself to give a *Gold Star* to Julie and Zahid for their clean code. He might forget, though. Hopefully not.

Ah, but are they done?

In fact, Julie and Zahid have only tested one multiple key combination. While it is impossible to test them all (why?), certainly they can do better. Here is a slightly more complete list of tests, given that they only have the two press methods.

```
    . . .
    @Test
    public void test53() {
            model.pressFive();
            model.pressThree();
            assertEquals(53, model.display());
    }
    @Test
    public void test55() {
            model.pressFive();
            model.pressFive();
            assertEquals(55, model.display());
    }
    @Test
    public void test355() {
            model.pressThree();
            model.pressFive();
            model.pressFive ();
            assertEquals(355, model.display());
    }
    . . .
```

Now they will have better confidence that they got it right. Hopefully they will remember to do this. The same CalculatorModel code passes all these tests.

The tests, of course, and their names, are very specific. And, again, the tests are independent, so the key presses in test55 don't affect the outcome of test355. The tests refer to different model objects.

Julie bumps into Zahid at the coffee shop.

Hi Zahid. I've been thinking about our project

Sure, me too.

It occurred to me that we could make the program more elegant by having actual *key* objects for the numeric keys. Each key could know its own value and fire off *accumulate* when sent the press message. Encapsulating the values.

Yeah, but why would we do that? I agree, it's more elegant, but we have a working program. All our tests pass. Seems like a complication for no benefit. The object behavior would be trivial.

Yes. Maybe an idea before its time. Let's see where the stories take us.

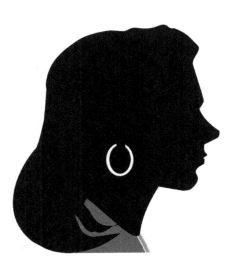

Objects Objects Objects

So far, the code is very simple and not wonderfully enlightening. The model has a field and a few methods. The only new thing for most of the readers might be how testing fits in to the process. It is about to get a bit more interesting.

The complete list of stories can be found at the end of the text, so we won't show the cards inline anymore. But the next story (Story 4, Operator Key) is clearly incomplete. What does it even mean? This is a situation in which the programmers need to have a discussion with the story owner, Dr. J, about what should happen when the + key is pressed. No addition can be done, since the second operand is not yet available when the plus key is pressed.

What has to happen, according to The Doctor, is that pressing the + key just sets the calculator up to accept the next operand. At some point we need to save the first operand, but this story doesn't make that explicit. In this case, the story owner can define what is intended by specifying a few tests. Dr J. knows how to write tests, of course, but not every story owner will. Here is the first test.

```
@Test
public void testSimplePlus() {
        model.pressThree();
        model.pressFive();
        model.pressPlus();
        assertEquals(35, model.display());
}
```

So, pressing + has no effect on the display, But the next numeric key pressed will change the display. It isn't accumulating *all* the numeric keys. Accumulation is reset at +, as the second test shows.

```
@Test
public void testComplexPlus() {
        model.pressThree();
        model.pressFive();
        model.pressPlus();
        assertEquals(35, model.display());
        model.pressFive();
        model.pressFive();
        assertEquals(55, model.display());
}
```

Of course the calculator will eventually need to have a way to store two operands for an operator like +. But that is something that can't be tested directly, since the fields that would hold them are private. Testing with JUnit can only test non-private things since the test class is separate from the model class. This separation is intentional and desirable. If the test and model classes are in the same package then you can test non-public things (e.g. default visibility), but not private fields and methods. Keep that in mind, but the solution is *not* to make things more visible. Rather, find ways to test the effects, not the fields themselves.

Can you improve the test above? Would additional assertions help? Should there be another test for minus?

Note that the story owner likely has a pretty specific idea about what he or she means by a story, but it may be hard to capture in a sentence or two. In some ways a story card is really just a contract to have a conversation between the customer and the developers. The understanding derived in the conversation is then captured in tests. This is very common in Agile Software Development.

Let's rejoin Julie and Zahid, back in the lab as they discuss this new story...

Hi Zahid, I had a talk with Dr. J about the operator key story. He said that hitting the + key doesn't change the display, but then pressing a numeric key starts a new operand.

Hmmm. OK. Why don't you type in a couple of tests for that and we'll see if I can make them pass.

OK. (types, as above) We just need a *pressPlus* method for the plus key. I may as well add the *pressPlus* to the model also. Aaaannnddd, run the tests. Red!

Good. Gee, I love to see that red bar. It forces me to do what I love – programming.

Don't go all ironic on me, now.

Actually, it clarifies the goal, so it really is a good thing.

Yeah, but how do we solve the problem here? Now the numeric keys have two different possible behaviors: accumulating and resetting.

Right. After + they reset, otherwise accumulate. Hmmm...

34

Maybe your idea about key objects fits here. The keys won't have trivial behavior now. And we also have two kinds of keys – numeric and operator.

So an Interface for the keys? With just a press method?

Sounds right. (creates a new Java interface) A new file in the same package.

```java
package juliezahid.calculator;

public interface Key {
    public void press();
}
```

And in the model class, create a couple of NumericKeys and update the pressThree and pressFive methods.

```java
private int display = 0;
private Key three = new NumericKey(3);
private Key five = new NumericKey(5);

public void pressThree() {
        three.press();
}
...
```

But we don't have a NumericKey class yet. You need to write that and make it implement Key. Where should we put it?

It may as well be an *inner class* in the CalculatorModel class, since it is only useful there. Right?

Sure, and it needs *accumulate* to be accessible, too. Go for it.

```java
private class NumericKey implements Key {
        private int value;

        public NumericKey(int value){
                this.value = value;
        }

        @Override
        public void press() {
                accumulate(value);
        }

}
```

OK. Let's run the tests. Ah. The old ones still pass so we haven't broken what we had, but the new ones still fail.

What we did was just refactoring, right?

Yep.

So, now for the main event. We have two behaviors in the press methods, so we need an IF, right? And a flag of some sort to test.

Wait, Dr. J had something to say about that in class. Let me check my notes. Ah. Polymorphism.

Alternative to IF

Delegate an action to another object rather than executing it directly.

--Strategy object

For each different action/behavior, use a separate object.

Strategies implement an interface.

So, we need a NumericStrategy interface, with a couple of implementations, one for each behavior.

OK. Here is the interface. (types)

```
package juliezahid.calculator;

public interface NumericStrategy {
    public void execute(int value);
}
```

We interrupt the story in progress for an important announcement.

What is wrong with an IF statement here? Actually nothing. In the following it will seem like Julie and Zahid are writing a lot more code than necessary, but they really won't be. It is just arranged a bit differently than you might be used to. In a situation like this a professional would just do what seems easiest at the time: probably an IF statement, testing a flag or expression. But we will later see that the same structure recurs in this program, as is true in most larger programs. At that point any extra effort here will get paid back with interest. So, stay tuned for an interesting plot twist.

But now, we are going to peek ahead at the road Julie and Zahid are traveling. They discovered that initially all the calculator "knew" how to do was accumulate. But when an operator key is pressed it must move to a new *state* that they will call *reset*. We can document this in a *State Transition Diagram* as follows. This diagram can be used to show you what sort of IF statement they would need to write, but also, important for us here, what sort of objects they need to build.

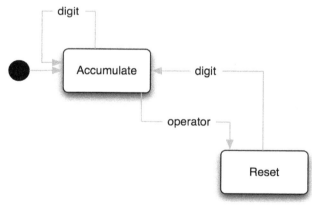

When a digit is pressed it continues to accumulate. It stays in the Accumulate *state, so* the action is to accumulate. Actions take place on the transitions.

When an operator is pressed it goes to the Reset state. Then the action will be different. (see below)

Also, in the Reset state, pressing a digit will send it back to the Accumulate state. Not all transitions are shown yet. What should happen if it is in the Reset state and an operator is pressed? Hmm...

Let's return to our programmers.

Julie: Why the parameter?

Zahid: Well, I think I've got it right. We have Key objects, right? And each key knows its own value, 3 or whatever. It will be the keys that execute the strategies so they can send their own value as the argument. Yes.

Hmmm. Pretty sure I follow, keep going. But we need two different strategy types, don't we? An accumulate strategy and a reset strategy. One for each behavior.

Yes, here is the first. Inner to the CalculatorModel.

```java
public class AccumulateStrategy implements NumericStrategy {
    @Override
    public void execute(int value) {
        accumulate(value);
    }
}
```

We also need one of these for the keys to execute. Like this...

```java
private NumericStrategy accumulate = new AccumulateStrategy();
```

It's a field of the model since all the numeric keys will share it.

And I need to change the *press* method in NumericKey to use this object instead of just firing accumulate directly. Like this...

```java
private class NumericKey implements Key {
        ...
        @Override
        public void press() {
                accumulate.execute(value);
        }
    }
```

Hmmm... Its starting to get complicated. Do we have any benefit yet?

Not yet, but look, we still pass all the old tests. Just a couple more changes to get the new ones. We need a ResetStrategy and a way to switch strategies when we press the equals key.

Since all the keys have the same strategy at any given time we can have a *currentStrategy* in the model.

That makes sense. You've been driving quite a while let me have a go to see if I've really got it.

Sure. (passes keyboard)

So, we need a new ResetStrategy class, though I'm not sure yet what to do in its execute method.

```java
private class ResetStrategy implements NumericStrategy {
        @Override
        public void execute(int value) {
                //TODO
        }
}
```

And a couple new fields, like this:

```java
private NumericStrategy accumulate = new AccumulateStrategy();
private NumericStrategy currentStrategy = accumulate;
private NumericStrategy reset = new ResetStrategy();
```

And then pressPlus just sets currentStrategy to the new reset strategy.

```java
public void pressPlus() {
        currentStrategy = reset;
}
```

Gotta fix up NumericKey too.

Right, when we *press* a numeric key it should execute the *current* strategy instead of always the accumulate strategy.

```
private class NumericKey implements Key {
        ...
        @Override
        public void press() {
                currentStrategy.execute(value);
        }
    }
```

Where are we? Do we pass the tests yet?

Nope. We haven't filled in ResetStrategy yet. I think that's the last step.

Let's see now. The current strategy gets set when we *pressPlus*, but it doesn't get executed until later when we press a numeric key. So the *reset* strategy should just put that key's value into the display, right?

Yes, but I think it also needs to set the currentStrategy back to accumulate for the next presses.

Ahhh... Sure.

Here is the current state of the CalculatorModel class.

```
package juliezahid.calculator;
public class CalculatorModel {

    private class ResetStrategy implements NumericStrategy {
            @Override
            public void execute(int value) {
                    display = value;
                    currentStrategy = accumulate;
            }
    }


    private class AccumulateStrategy implements NumericStrategy {
            @Override
            public void execute(int value) {
                    display = display * 10 + value;
            }
    }


    private class NumericKey implements Key {
            private int value;
            public NumericKey(int value){
                    this.value = value;
            }
            @Override
            public void press() {
                    currentStrategy.execute(value);
            }
    }

    private int display = 0;
    private Key three = new NumericKey(3);
    private Key five = new NumericKey(5);
    private NumericStrategy accumulate = new AccumulateStrategy();
    private NumericStrategy currentStrategy = accumulate;
    private NumericStrategy reset = new ResetStrategy();
    public int display() {
            return display;
```

```
        }

        public void pressThree() {
                three.press();
        }

        public void pressFive() {
                five.press();
        }

        public void pressPlus() {
                currentStrategy = reset;
        }

}
```

Note that they have also dropped the *accumulate* method and just moved it's code into AccumulateStrategy.

This code now passes the tests for Story 4. Dr. J approves.

What Julie and Zahid have used here is called the **Strategy Design Pattern**. A *design pattern* is a standard way of solving a common problem. In this case the problem is one of switching between behaviors in an object (here, the NumericKey objects). The behavior is *delegated* to another object (*currentStrategy*) which has one of two possible values, *accumulate* and *reset*. Those values can sometimes be instances from the same class but here they are from two different classes implementing the same interface.

Delegation is a Big Idea in Object-Oriented Programming.

Design patterns also form a vocabulary of design ideas that are useful in a team's discussion of a development problem. "Hey George, this is a good place to apply a *Strategy*."

The calculator still doesn't perform the addition, though. That has to wait until they implement the equals key. Onward.

A Note on Encapsulation

Purists will complain that Julie and Zahid haven't built *real* objects. The inner classes and the CalculatorModel are definitely not completely encapsulated. For example, the ResetStrategy class specifically references and changes the *display* and *currentStrategy* fields of the containing class. Information leaks into the contained object, though not outward.

```
private class ResetStrategy implements NumericStrategy {
        @Override
        public void execute(int value) {
            display = value;
            currentStrategy = accumulate;
        }
}
```

The inner classes and the CalculatorModel are tightly bound to each other. The code would get very messy if we try to "correct" this. For example, to make ResetStrategy an independent, top-level, class we would need to also provide a mutator method (a *setter*) for the *display* field of CalculatorModel and it would need sufficient visibility. But an object such as our model should never have such a visible mutator.

But note that these classes are really just *parts* of the CalculatorModel. They have no independent existence. There is little benefit in full encapsulation in such a situation, since they are working within a single class and they are built within one team. The encapsulation boundary here is CalculatorModel. The inner classes are just implementation details. You would have a hard life if your brain were completely encapsulated from, say, your left foot. This is part of the concept of piecemeal growth. The technique leads to an *organic* whole, not to a loose collection of independent parts.

Our students are back in the lab for the Equals Key Story This one will actually make the application seem like a calculator.

Zahid: OK. Story 5 requires the equals and minus keys. Shall we do them separately or all at once?

We can delay that decision until we know a bit more. Let me write a test for this story. First equals after just plus.

```
@Test
public void testEquals() {
        model.pressThree();
        model.pressFive();
        model.pressPlus();
        assertEquals(35, model.display());
        model.pressFive();
        model.pressFive();
        assertEquals(55, model.display());
        model.pressEquals();
        assertEquals(90, model.display());
}
```

Looks good. The minus test could be the same but with *pressMinus* and a result of -20.

Right. Driving back to you you, sir! Now, what do we need to do here?

Well, since we will have two operators keys, we probably need objects for them. And notice that the test says that the action of the operator gets actually done when the equals key gets pressed, not the plus and minus keys. So how do we know what to do when we press equals?

How about this? The operator key gets pressed *earlier* than the equals key. Like 55 – 32 =. Yes?

So when the operator key gets pressed we just remember the key itself, a *currentOperator*. Then, when we *pressEquals*, we do the action of the *currentOperator*. Something like delegation, again.

OK. Let me start with that and work backwards.

```
public void pressEquals() {
        currentOperator.operate();
}
```

So operator keys *operate*. Good.

We have several kinds of operators but they have the same actions, so we want an interface for OperatorKey, I think. If it extends Key then we have the *press* method included already.

```
package juliezahid.calculator;

public interface OperatorKey extends Key {
    public void operate();
}
```

I think we need to back up a bit here. To do an operation we need two operands, left and right, but we only have the *display*. But we can solve that with another field to save the display while we accumulate the second. We know we are done with the first one when we press the operator key.

So, something like this in *pressPlus*?

```
public void pressPlus() {
        currentStrategy = reset;
        oldDisplay = display;
    }
```

Yes, but it should really be in the press method of a new Plus Key object, I think. And you need to remember *that* object as the currentOperator, too.

Oh, right. And then the body of *pressPlus* just becomes *plus.press*().

```
private class Plus implements OperatorKey {

        @Override
        public void press() {
                oldDisplay = display;
                currentStrategy = reset;
                currentOperator = this;
        }

        @Override
        public void operate() {
                //TODO
        }

}
```

So, when we press the plus key we remember the old operand, reset the accumulate strategy to start picking up the new operand, and remember plus was pressed. Whew.

Now I just need to define *operate* in this class. Obvious, I think. Give the model a new display.

```
@Override
public void operate() {
        display = oldDisplay + display;
}
```

You have to set up the new fields, though.

Oh, right.

```
private OperatorKey plus = new Plus();
private OperatorKey currentOperator = plus;
```

Wait. Why is the default value of the currentOperator set to *plus*?

How about null?

Doc will skin us if you do that. How about a **Null Object**. Remember that pattern from last month, and all the trouble we had catching null pointer exceptions?

Hmmm... yes. An OperatorKey that has an empty operation. Sounds better.

```
private class NoOperator implements OperatorKey {

        @Override
        public void press() {
                // nothing
        }

        @Override
        public void operate() {
                // nothing
        }

    }
...
    private OperatorKey plus = new Plus();
    private OperatorKey noOperator = new NoOperator();
    private OperatorKey currentOperator = noOperator;
```

And now I think the code should pass the test for plus. Try it.

Yay. Green bar. But let me finish up with the Minus key and the other test. Pretty sure I subtract *display* from *oldDisplay*, not the other way round.

Right. Do it. Just copy Plus and fix it up. Oh, and create a new *minus* object too, of course.

Here is the latest CalculatorModel. It satisfies the first five stories.

```
package juliezahid.calculator;
public class CalculatorModel {

    private class Minus implements OperatorKey {
            @Override
            public void press() {
                    oldDisplay = display;
                    currentStrategy = reset;
                    currentOperator = this;
            }
            @Override
            public void operate() {
                    display = oldDisplay - display;
            }
    }

    private class NoOperator implements OperatorKey {
            @Override
            public void press() {
                    // nothing
            }
            @Override
            public void operate() {
                    // nothing
            }
    }

    private class Plus implements OperatorKey {
            @Override
            public void press() {
                    oldDisplay = display;
                    currentStrategy = reset;
                    currentOperator = this;
            }
    }
```

```java
        @Override
        public void operate() {
                display = oldDisplay + display;
        }
}


private class ResetStrategy implements NumericStrategy {
        @Override
        public void execute(int value) {
                display = value;
                currentStrategy = accumulate;
        }
}


private class AccumulateStrategy implements NumericStrategy {
        @Override
        public void execute(int value) {
                display = display * 10 + value;
        }
}


private class NumericKey implements Key {
        private int value;

        public NumericKey(int value){
                this.value = value;
        }

        @Override
        public void press() {
                currentStrategy.execute(value);
        }
}

private int display = 0;
private int oldDisplay = 0;
private Key three = new NumericKey(3);
private Key five = new NumericKey(5);
```

```
        private NumericStrategy accumulate = new AccumulateStrategy();
        private NumericStrategy currentStrategy = accumulate;
        private NumericStrategy reset = new ResetStrategy();
        private OperatorKey plus = new Plus();
        private OperatorKey noOperator = new NoOperator();
        private OperatorKey currentOperator = noOperator;
        private OperatorKey minus = new Minus();

        public int display() {
                return display;
        }

        public void pressThree() {
                three.press();
        }

        public void pressFive() {
                five.press();
        }

        public void pressPlus() {
                plus.press();
        }

        public void pressMinus() {
                minus.press();
        }

        public void pressEquals() {
                currentOperator.operate();
        }
}
```

Note that the longest method body has three statements. Every method is about as simple as it is possible to be. The only statements used have been assignment and message passing. A few operators, such as + and *new* have been used, also.

The State Transition Diagram that Julie and Zahid have just implemented now looks something like this:

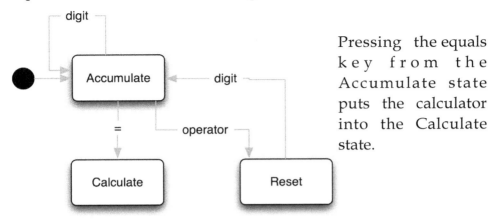

Pressing the equals key from the Accumulate state puts the calculator into the Calculate state.

Actually, that isn't quite true, though it gives the correct idea. Note that pressing the equals key didn't change the strategy, which is being used to represent the state. It just performed the calculation. The calculator was left in the Accumulate state. Will that be a problem? Can it be fixed easily?

But the stories will also need to address transitions from The Calculate state as well. What should happen if you are in that state, having just pressed equals, and then a digit key, is pressed? An operator? What should happen if equals is pressed again? What *does* happen? How can you determine that?

Transitions happen when some event, such as a key press, occurs.

Examine this transition diagram. We have three kinds of keys: digit, operator, and equals. From the Accumulate state we have addressed transitions for each of these kinds of keys. What about the other states? So, such a diagram can help you see what is still missing in the application.

A transition diagram like this could be the beginning of the development of an architecture for the program, within the overall MVC structure. Julie and Zahid seem not to have thought of that, though. Perhaps Dr. J should talk about it in class. Maybe he will.

Polymorphism

The code just above represents the heart of our example and we have reached the core of our message. The various Key objects required different behavior at different times. Rather than using IF statements to choose an action, the Keys delegate the action to a separate object and the object reference changes with the state of the computation. The *Key* objects are polymorphic: they have *many forms*. But each Strategy object only "knows" one of the actions.

Each of the parts we built is very, almost trivially, simple. There is complexity here, but only in the interactions among the objects. The key idea is **Delegation** to strategy objects. There are some deeper tricks available beyond Strategy, but not discussed here.

If you have experience programming with classes and objects, notice what we have *not* done: build complex general purpose classes, decided on at the beginning of the project. Instead, each inner class was purpose-built for its task. They are built *just in time*. The classes may not be especially general or reusable in another program, but they are useful here. Since each of the classes is so small (just a few methods) each can be understood easily. Each captures *one* idea. We have simple classes with simple methods.

We have a few more ingredients, but the flavor of the task is set.

Here is the path to success with polymorphic programming: programming with a minimum of ad hoc decisions in the code.

a) Find yourself in a situation in which one of two or more behaviors is possible. (*accumulate* or *reset*)

b) Build a separate object for each behavior. They may be different objects in the same class, or objects from different classes implementing the same interface. (e.g. Strategies)

c) Find a way to bring the correct object to bear as needed. (Here, it is when the operator key was pressed, and when it was later executed.)

Why is it important to program this way? Well, it isn't essential, of course. Many programs get written with a lot of IF and SWITCH statements, even in Object-Oriented languages. But in many ways the code here is cleaner than the alternative. If you don't have IF statements you don't have to worry about trying to understand long IF and ELSE parts that have IF statements embedded within them, for example. Those are especially difficult when the parts are long or the nesting is deep. In a sense, rather than helper methods to handle this situation, we use *helper objects*, instead.

But the real reason is deeper. If you have a situation in which a decision (one of two or more behaviors) needs to be made in any large program then it is fairly likely that one of two situations will occur elsewhere. First, the same decision structure may occur again, though with different behaviors needed. In this case, the IF programmer rebuilds the IF statement structure to test the same expression or flag. But the polymorphic programmer adds a new method to the interface defining the behaviors and implements that method once for each alternative.

The other situation is that the problem changes and you need new behaviors, or a third or fourth alternative. Here the IF programmer has to find the, perhaps many, IF statements testing that particular state and fix them up *consistently*. But the polymorphic programmer just creates a new object for each new behavior. The polymorphic solution is more compact and localized within the program, leading to fewer errors of omission – forgetting to do something essential. The tools aren't very good at finding and distinguishing IF statements in a large program that uses them extensively, but they *are* good at forcing you to implement all methods of an interface.

Actually, a strategy object acts like a flag, but it has behavior. It can directly execute that behavior rather than having to guard it with a test. Two objects, two different behaviors. A Big Idea.

A complete description of the contrast between polymorphic and ad hoc decision making can be found online at http://joe.fed.wiki.org.

You can also explore these ideas in Chapter 4 of *Karel J Robot: A Gentle Introduction to the Art of Object-Oriented Programming in Java*.

Polymorphism has now been used twice in the program. The behavior of the numeric keys is polymorphic since the actions depend on the *currentStrategy*. So, instead of setting a flag telling us that an operator key was pressed and then checking that flag to decide how the numeric key should behave, we just let the numeric key delegate the action to one or the other of the strategy objects.

Similarly, the equals key is now polymorphic since it just performs the operation of the *currentOperator*, either *plus* or *minus*. This means that we didn't need to set a multi-valued flag telling us which operator key was pressed and then later check that flag, probably in a SWITCH statement, and perform an addition, subtraction, etc. as needed. In effect, the operator key *itself* acts like a flag, except that it has behavior. Therefore we don't need to test, and then choose the correct behavior; each operator key knows its own proper behavior. So *pressEquals* just delegates to that operator key via the *currentOperator* reference variable.

But note, if we had solved the problems here with flags and IF and SWITCH statements, we would have written the same action code. What we have above as method bodies of our strategies would just become the bodies of the IF and ELSE clauses of the tests made for the numeric keys. Likewise, the bodies of the operate methods of classes Plus and Minus (and others later) would be the various CASE clauses of a SWITCH used to test the flag for the operation of the equals key.

In the following pages we shall see that one of these decision structures will recur in this application. If we had solved our problems with IF and SWITCH we would need to reproduce the same structure in that new code. But if we forget a clause or a case, our application is broken. It isn't such a big thing in a simple case, but if a SWITCH has many cases, or the IF structure is nested in some way, it can be a challenging problem to get it right. Testing will help, of course, but the polymorphic solution we outline above makes it much harder to forget a case since the tools insist that when we implement an interface we implement every method. Watch for the recurrence and see if you notice it when it arises.

Back to the students, once again...

Julie: Dr. J seems to like our code.
I guess we are on the right track.

Yes, makes me feel good. What's next?

Two wrinkles about equals. If you hit equals twice, nothing new happens and if you hit equals when there isn't any operator, nothing happens either. Your turn to write tests, I think.

```java
@Test
public void testDoubleEquals() {
        model.pressThree();
        model.pressMinus();
        assertEquals(3, model.display());
        model.pressFive();
        assertEquals(5, model.display());
        model.pressEquals();
        assertEquals(-2, model.display());
        model.pressEquals();
        assertEquals(-2, model.display());
}

@Test
public void testEqualsWhenNoOperator() {
        model.pressFive();
        assertEquals(5, model.display());
        model.pressEquals();
        assertEquals(5, model.display());
        model.pressEquals();
        assertEquals(5, model.display());
}
```

Whoa. That was a happy surprise. Test with no operator already passes. Nothing to do?

I guess that is because we initialize the *currentOperator* with *noOperator*, so it just doesn't change anything when invoked.

But the other test fails. The test says -2 was expected at the end, but 5 was the value.

(thinks...)

(thinks...)

OK, when we press equals the second time, when the *currentOperator* is *minus*, we re-execute *minus.operate*.

Riiiight. And we re-set the *display* to *oldDisplay* – *display*. And *oldDisplay* is still 3 and the *display* is -2, so we get 3 - (-2) or 5.

So how do we fix it? Fiddle with *oldDisplay*?

No, I think we just set *currentOperator* to *noOperator* at the end of *operate*. Same in class Plus.

Yep. That did it. Green in 10 minutes.

Just to emphasize, when we run the tests, all of them are run, not just the latest tests. This is called *regression* testing. Here is a version of Julie and Zahid's test file. The current CalculatorModel passes **all** these. Adding new features hasn't broken what they did before. They didn't need to back up, but that is largely serendipity. In the real world, things change or the stories are originally inconsistent so you might need to revisit code (and get the stories unified, of course). But the tests still tell you what works and what doesn't.

```java
package juliezahid.calculator;
import static org.junit.Assert.*;
import org.junit.Before;
import org.junit.Test;

public class CalculatorModelTest {
    private CalculatorModel model;

    @Before
    public void setUp() throws Exception {
        model = new CalculatorModel();
    }

    @Test
    public void test() {
        assertEquals(0, model.display());
    }

    @Test
    public void testSingle3Key() {
        model.pressThree();
        assertEquals(3, model.display());
    }

    @Test
    public void testSingle5Key() {
        model.pressFive();
        assertEquals(5, model.display());
    }
```

```java
@Test
public void test53() {
        model.pressFive();
        model.pressThree();
        assertEquals(53, model.display());
}

@Test
public void test55() {
        model.pressFive();
        model.pressFive();
        assertEquals(55, model.display());
}

@Test
public void test35() {
        model.pressThree();
        model.pressFive();
        assertEquals(35, model.display());
}

@Test
public void testSimplePlus() {
        model.pressThree();
        model.pressFive();
        model.pressPlus();
        assertEquals(35, model.display());
}

@Test
public void testComplexPlus() {
        model.pressThree();
        model.pressFive();
        model.pressPlus();
        assertEquals(35, model.display());
        model.pressFive();
        model.pressFive();
        assertEquals(55, model.display());
}
```

```java
@Test
public void testEquals() {
        model.pressThree();
        model.pressFive();
        model.pressPlus();
        assertEquals(35, model.display());
        model.pressFive();
        model.pressFive();
        assertEquals(55, model.display());
        model.pressEquals();
        assertEquals(90, model.display());
}

@Test
public void testEqualsAfterMinus() {
        model.pressThree();
        model.pressFive();
        model.pressMinus();
        assertEquals(35, model.display());
        model.pressFive();
        model.pressFive();
        assertEquals(55, model.display());
        model.pressEquals();
        assertEquals(-20, model.display());
}

@Test
public void testDoubleEquals() {
        model.pressThree();
        model.pressMinus();
        assertEquals(3, model.display());
        model.pressFive();
        assertEquals(5, model.display());
        model.pressEquals();
        assertEquals(-2, model.display());
        model.pressEquals();
        assertEquals(-2, model.display());
}
```

```
@Test
public void testEqualsWhenNoOperator() {
        model.pressThree();
        model.pressFive();
        assertEquals(35, model.display());
        model.pressEquals();
        assertEquals(35, model.display());
        model.pressEquals();
        assertEquals(35, model.display());
}

}
```

Many of these tests were "written" by just copying an existing test and adding to it or changing it slightly. Copy-Paste-Fixup.

Note that we make assertions *within* each test also, not just as the last statement. So if a test fails we need to look to see the statement at which it failed. It won't always be the last. The individual test doesn't continue past the first failure. But tests are independent so the other tests are still run even if some fail.

Another advantage of coding like this, driven by testing, is that you will be led to do just enough to make the tests pass. You won't be as tempted to just write code hoping something nice will happen. You won't be tempted to get ahead of the need, writing speculatively. That often leads to errors. One way to make fewer errors is to write less code. Just enough to get the job done.

If you prefer a style in which each test has only one assertion, it is easy to break a single test into several, with each test ending in an assertion, but not containing others.

We are going to leave Julie and Zahid for a bit so that you, the reader, can have some fun building Stories 7, 8, and 9. You can download the code up to the current state, along with a complete test file through Story 9.

You can also download the code as an Eclipse Project archive that you can import directly. Note that the tests for Stories 8 and 9 have been commented out in the project version to help you get started on just Story 7.

http://csis.pace.edu/~bergin/polymorphismBook/Downloads.html

The files included in both versions are:

CalculatorModel.java

CalculatorModelTest.java

Key.java

NumericStrategy.java

OperatorKey.java

Get the code running and build stories 7, 8, and 9, passing the included tests.

The test for Story 7 can be passed by adding a single line of code to an existing method and the others by adding a method or two for each. The best way to do this is Pair Programming with a buddy. As you read this, the real-life Julie and Zahid have graduated, of course, so won't be available. You'll have to find your own partner.

We rejoin our characters, Julie and Zahid, about to start on Story 10 ...

Zahid: OK. back to work. Those last three weren't too bad. Is Dr. J getting soft?

Ha. Not likely. What do we have next? Continuing a calculation after hitting equals. Story 10.

Ah, so you can get intermediate results and keep going. Show me a test so I can code, code, code.

Here ya go, buddy.

```java
@Test
public void testContinuedCalculation() {
        model.pressThree();
        model.pressPlus();
        assertEquals(3, model.display());
        model.pressFive();
        assertEquals(5, model.display());
        model.pressEquals();
        assertEquals(8, model.display());
        model.pressMinus();
        model.pressFive();
        model.pressEquals();
        assertEquals(3, model.display());
}
```

And run the tests and …

Green. Wait. What? Again?

Nothing to do. Unbelievable. He really is getting soft. Check it off.

While the programmers had nothing at all to do to handle Story 10, it might not have happened that way. It depends on how they solved earlier problems, not considering this case. They might have had a lot of work to do here, depending on the nature of the earlier decisions they made.

But, if nothing else, there is now an additional set of tests that will be maintained as they progress.

Julie and Zahid have, throughout this exercise, made a stunning sequence of correct, if serendipitous, decisions. That isn't too realistic in practice, but the author didn't want to make the book too long. In the real world, unlike this fiction, you sometimes go wrong and need to back up. Life is messy. Tests add some order.

An important aspect of programming in this style is that you will typically write more test code than application code, at least until you start to write a Graphical User Interface. GUIs often require a lot of code. But for now, note that the application itself, including the interfaces in separate files, requires about 170 lines of code, but the test file is about 100 lines longer.

So, does testing slow you down or speed you up? Those who use this method firmly believe it speeds you up. You don't have to correct as many bugs. You don't have to sit there trying to figure out messy code. Not as much or as often, usually. It isn't the typing that makes programming hard, of course. But one of the reasons we have so little program code is that this technique naturally led Julie and Zahid to write just enough code to satisfy the need. They didn't decide early on that they needed Key objects and spend a lot of time trying to develop a general Key class that *might* be useful, but likely had additional, unused, features (called *cruft*). In fact, the Key classes (such as Minus) are *private* inner classes, so are explicitly excluded from general use. And polymorphism kept the code as simple as possible.

One skill every programmer needs is to know how fast they can build something so they can estimate for a client. A way to gain that skill is to record tasks and elapsed times in a personal notebook.

Zahid and Julie continue...

Zahid: Well, here we are again. Just a couple more stories.

Yep. It's been fun, too. What next?

Ah, yes, multiple operators:

53 + 3 + 5 should give 61

I can't believe we didn't see that earlier. At least he says to ignore precedence. That will make multiplication easier. We should test subtraction too, I think.

```java
@Test
public void testMultipleOperators() {
        model.pressThree();
        model.pressPlus();
        model.pressThree();
        model.pressPlus();
        assertEquals(6, model.display());
        model.pressThree();
        model.pressPlus();
        assertEquals(9, model.display());
        model.pressThree();
        model.pressMinus();
        assertEquals(12, model.display());
        model.pressFive();
        model.pressEquals();
        assertEquals(7, model.display());
}
```

Well, the code certainly fails that test. Fails early and often. At least you get to drive this time.

Yeah, thanks, pal.

Wait. Look at the test. When we press an operator like plus, the operator has to get executed.

Hmmm. No, actually the *previous* operator get executed. Just like when we *pressEquals*. When we *pressMinus* the previous addition get executed.

Ah. The test points them to the solution. Very nice.

So pressing an operator key has to also do what *pressEquals* does. That's the key to this one.

But look at the model. The *press* methods of Plus and Minus are identical. I think the same will be true for multiplication and division. Maybe we should refactor this a bit before we continue. Factor the common code to a superclass.

Like this, with an abstract class...

```
private abstract class AllOperators implements OperatorKey{
        @Override
        public void press() {
                oldDisplay = display;
                currentStrategy = reset;
                currentOperator = this;
        }
}

private class Minus extends AllOperators {
        @Override
        public void operate() {
                display = oldDisplay - display;
                currentOperator = noOperator;
        }
}

private class Plus extends AllOperators {
        @Override
        public void operate() {
                display = oldDisplay + display;
                currentOperator = noOperator;
        }
}
```

Yeah. The *say it once* principle.

Now back to Story 11. *PressEquals* tells the current operator to *operate* and sets the strategy to the *reset* strategy. Can we just add that to *press* in AllOperators?

Hmmm. The strategy is already set there, so just add the *operate* message...

```
@Override
public void press() {
        currentOperator.operate();
        oldDisplay = display;
        currentStrategy = reset;
        currentOperator = this;
}
```

OK. Not so good. We pass the new test but now the equals after *plus minus* test breaks. An old test from Story 8.

```
@Test
public void testEqualsAfterPlusMinus() {
        model.pressThree();
        model.pressFive();
        model.pressPlus(); // correct a wrong operator press
        model.pressMinus();
        assertEquals(35, model.display());
        model.pressFive();
        model.pressFive();
        assertEquals(55, model.display());
        model.pressEquals();
        assertEquals(-20, model.display());
}
```

It says we got 70 there instead of 35. Hmmm... We executed the *plus* when the minus was pressed instead of replacing it.

Look, when we *pressPlus*, the display is copied to *oldDisplay*. So when we *pressMinus* and execute the plus, both have 35, so we get 70.

Suppose we delay copying the display until later. Say when we execute the reset strategy?

```java
private abstract class AllOperators implements OperatorKey{
        @Override
        public void press() {
                currentOperator.operate();
                currentStrategy = reset;
                currentOperator = this;
        }
}


private class ResetStrategy implements NumericStrategy {
        @Override
        public void execute(int value) {
                oldDisplay = display;
                display = value;
                currentStrategy = accumulate;
        }
}
```

Perfect. Green. It's the last moment before the display will be replaced. Good thinking.

We seem to be having more interactions now. I think we need to go over the logic carefully and add a few more tests.

I need to break. I have a tough session at the gym in an hour.

OK. I need to research my philosophy paper a bit, too. Descartes. *Discourse on Method.*

> A better place to take a break is just after you write a new *failing* test. Your subconscious will work on the solution while you're away *and* you'll have a clear goal when you return to work.

● ● ●

They later went to visit Dr. J to ask for advice. He suggested that they, indeed, write a few more tests to see if they can think of a way to break their code. They did, but didn't find anything.

Can *you* find any bugs? Try writing more tests to see what works and what, if anything, doesn't. Do they have the right tests?

Note that the way to exercise this code is through the test structure. It doesn't have a *main* function anywhere. It was meant to be a model, after all, not a complete application. It could be combined with one or more views and a controller to be a complete application.

We will leave Julie and Zahid to finish their work, and leave Story 12 to you. They will do it themselves, of course, and submit their work to Dr. J, who will, hopefully, reward them lavishly.

To do Story 12, you will have to do some explorations in order to do something sensible with division. The story reminds us that the calculator only produces integers, not decimals. We also haven't explored topics like correct error handling (Exceptions) for division by zero, since the purpose was to explore Polymorphism and Story Driven Development. JUnit has help for that, also.

Also, at the end of Page 38, we left a question unanswered. Is that covered in these stories? What would be a good story for that? How would you implement it?

Note that a good approach is the principle of *No Code Without A Failing Test*. Don't just try to program the CalculatorModel. Write tests first to capture your understanding of what should happen. Then, but only then, update the model to make your tests pass. So, even something so simple and obvious as putting in an 8 key requires one or, preferably, more tests.

And if you write the tests first, then you are testing whether you build what you think you *should build*. If you write the test after you write the code then you are testing only whether you built what you *did build*. Much less valuable.

Remember that you don't have control over the Stories themselves. They are owned by other people. If you have problems with them you need to go back to the owners for changes. Maybe they are unclear or you just don't understand them. Possibly they contradict earlier stories. Ask for clarification. You can, and should, suggest changes, of course. Sometimes you can suggest a simpler way to achieve the story owner's goals.

Oh, and try to write *beautiful*, not just correct, code. Think of programming as writing poetry, not shopping lists. Dr. J gives Gold Stars for that! And you'll sleep better, too.

More

Julie: The Doctor says we have a problem.

Dr who?

No, the Other Doctor. He says we used the wrong test for Story 9. But we can fix it up and he'll grade it again. We used a test something like this:

```
@Test
public void testSimpleClearEntry(){
        model.pressFive();
        model.pressPlus();
        model.pressClearEntry();
        assertEquals(0, model.display());
        model.pressThree();
        assertEquals(3, model.display());
        model.pressEquals();
        assertEquals(3, model.display());
}
```

But we had already pressed plus before the clear entry. We should have cleared the second operand, not the first. It should still be five.

Oh, right. Ah well. So the test should be like this, instead?

```
@Test
public void testSimpleClearEntry(){
        model.pressFive();
        model.pressPlus();
        model.pressClearEntry();
        assertEquals(5, model.display());
        model.pressThree();
        assertEquals(3, model.display());
        model.pressEquals();
        assertEquals(8, model.display());
}
```

Right. Well, let's get busy. Who's driving.

Well, since you came up with the issue, why not let me work on its solution? Our old solution was just to set the *display* to 0 in *clearEntry*, right?

Yes, and that can't work anymore since the display still holds the first operand. So, sometimes *clearEntry* sets *display* to 0 and sometimes it doesn't.

Sounds like...

Polymorphism

Polymorphism

Right, but where?

Well, when we've just pressed an operator key we shouldn't do anything. Otherwise clear the display.

Right, again. But that is just when we switch strategies. Maybe this should become a new method of *NumericStrategy*. Then *clearEntry* can just delegate to the currentStrategy. Like this...

```
package juliezahid.calculator;

public interface NumericStrategy {
    public void execute(int value);
    public void clearEntry();
}
```

And in the model...

```
public void pressClearEntry() {
        currentStrategy.clearEntry();
    }
```

Right. So it becomes a no-op in the ResetStrategy class and clears *display* in AccumulateStrategy.

Yes, like this.

```
private class ResetStrategy implements NumericStrategy {
        @Override
        public void execute(int value) {
                oldDisplay = display;
                display = value;
                currentStrategy = accumulate;
        }
        @Override
        public void clearEntry() {
        //      nothing
        }
}

private class AccumulateStrategy implements NumericStrategy {
        @Override
        public void execute(int value) {
                display = display * 10 + value;
        }

        @Override
        public void clearEntry() {
                display = 0;
        }
}
```

Yes. And I like that you document our intention that the body is empty in *ResetStrategy*.

Yeah. Trick I learned from The Doctor.

Couple of other tests need to be made consistent with this too.

Retrospective

After the project was completed, Dr. J held a discussion session with the class in which he shared some ideas about the code and the process. A more formal project review is called a *Retrospective*. It captures the knowledge of what worked and what didn't, to help the *next* project succeed. It often deals mostly with process, but here he focused on the resulting code since the pairing went well.

Dr. J noted that classes such as ResetStrategy have no fields; they are *stateless*. They are *Immutable*, since there is no state to change. Without state there is likely no need for more than a single object in the class: they are *Singletons*. There are simple techniques for enforcing the Immutable and Singleton properties of an object when required. He suggested the students explore these two ideas, and their tradeoffs, online. A program with a high proportion of Immutable objects is easier to reason about, since the state of such an object is the same as the state with which it is created: Another Big Idea. Mutable Singletons have some drawbacks, however.

Dr. J also mentioned that nearly all of the fields of CalculatorModel could be marked *final,* as they are constants. The fields that can't be final include *currentOperator* and *currentStrategy,* since changing those is fundamental to this way of programming. The advantage of using *final,* even within these inner classes is that you will be warned immediately if you, mistakenly, set *currentStrategy* to point to a newly created object when all you need is the existing value. It also permits the compiler to emit more efficient code. The inner classes can also be *final*: no subclassing allowed.

Note that the two display fields might better be collected into an object so they can be managed together. If that is done, none of the fields directly used are primitives (such as *int*). That is a good thing, since you then have more control as a programmer. Primitives have properties defined by the language, while objects have properties defined by the programmer.

The NumericKey objects are also Immutable and never modified. They have no mutators. You certainly don't want the five key to suddenly represent the number eight. It is useful to enforce immutability explicitly, if for no other reason than to make your intent clear.

There was also discussion of *complexity* during the retrospective. The calculator project itself has a certain amount of *essential* complexity. Keys do different things at different times, for example, however you build it. Most large projects have a great deal of essential complexity. But in programming with Polymorphism, the students didn't introduce additional, *inessential*, complexity in the code itself. The complexity remains in the problem, not the solution, since each piece is so easy to understand. This, in general, is also a Big Idea: Don't introduce inessential complexity.

The Doctor spent some time showing the State Transition Diagrams at various points in the program's development. Had the students noticed the advantages of such diagrams along the way it might have clarified things for them. But it would have been wrong of them to just take that idea and implement a complete program based on a diagram of their own design. It is the story owner who owns the project, not the developers. What should happen when, for example, an operator key is pressed in the Reset state is up to the customer (story owner) to decide, not the programmers. But it is the programmer's responsibility to raise the issue with the customer and make suggestions of alternatives and their consequences. When developing for someone else it is possible to be *too* creative.

There are some Decision/Selection problems that are difficult to solve with pure polymorphism. Sometimes, however, a single IF statement or SWITCH can set the conditions for later effective use of polymorphism. But it is useful, just for learning, to try to get along without them altogether. That will help you learn to be creative in a good way.

Conclusions...

What Julie and Zahid have been doing is called the *Polymorphism Étude*. Write a program with no ad hoc selection: no IF or SWITCH statements. That is a useful exercise for learning, but I don't want to suggest that it is the only way to program. In fact, a professional programmer might reasonably use IF statements for much of what we have done here. In particular, the first time you come to a decision point in the code, two or more behaviors, it is perfectly fine to solve the issue with an IF or SWITCH. But if you revisit that decision structure later in the program, as they just did in revisiting Story 9, you might want to replace it with polymorphic, rather than ad hoc decision making. The locality of the code changes. Some things that were far apart are then close together (within a class) and some things that were close together are now farther apart. But since it is the actions that are brought together, it aids maintainability. In the future it is less likely that you will forget to build a case with the polymorphic solution than with the ad hoc decisions. See http://joe.fed.wiki.org.

But even beyond polymorphism, the lesson here is to grow your programs organically using piecemeal growth. Develop them one key concept at a time rather than trying to build them all at once. Get *one* thing working and tested, or rather tested and working, before moving on. Let tests drive the development. Refactor when you think it will help you consolidate. Tailor each part you build to the task at hand. Avoid speculation. Julie and Zahid did all of that extremely well. Their communication and cooperation was also extraordinary. Bravo.

And get frequent feedback from the sponsor/owner of the program. In the real world it is a customer who pays your bills, after all.

But, if you haven't gained the skill to program polymorphism yet, I strongly recommend you spend some time at it. As the kids say, or did, this is **kewl**. Geek cred.

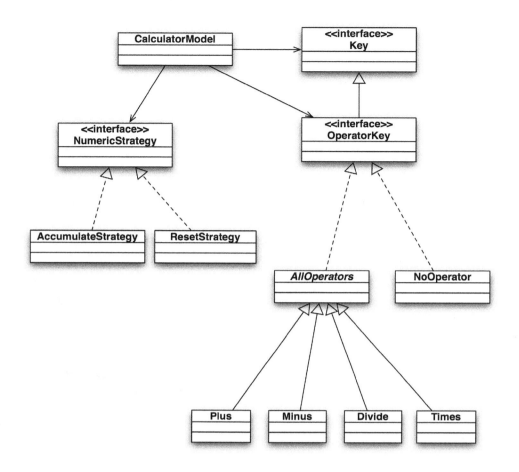

Above is the class diagram of the final program. It shows the relationships between the classes in UML (Unified Modeling Language) style. Note that there is no concrete class inheritance here at all. UML is often used as part of the design process when you work from a complete description of a project or try to create an overall design. In an incremental development, such as here, it is also useful for documentation of the result. We omit the fields and operations from the diagram.

NumericKey isn't shown. Can you add it? You will need two arrows.

The Stories

1. Zero Display: Create a calculator that will give you its display. A new calculator should have a display of 0.

2. Single Numeric Key: Give the calculator keys like 5 and 3. When you hit a single key the value of the key should "show" in the display.

3. Accumulate: If you press a sequence of number keys, the results should accumulate in the display.

4. Operator Key: Give the calculator a + key that eventually adds the results of two operands. The sum won't be actually performed until the = key is pressed. Other operator keys will be added later (-, *, /).

5. Equals Key: Give the calculator an = key that performs any outstanding operation and clears for a new calculation. Also implement a minus key to be sure you have the correct associativity.

6. Multiple Equals: Pressing = a second time will not repeat the operation. Display is unchanged. Pressing = when there is no outstanding operation will be ignored.

7. Multiple Calculations: After completing a computation it should be possible to carry out another computation immediately.

8. Clear All: Give the calculator a *Clear* key that will clear any outstanding operations, just as if it were turned off then on again. The display is 0. If you press an operator key, say minus, immediately after pressing another, the second operator will replace the first.

9. Clear Entry: Give the calculator a *ClearEntry* key that will clear the current operand, but leave outstanding operations in place. The display should show 0.

10. Continued Calculation: Pressing an operator immediately after equals will continue the current calculation.

11. Multiple Operators: An expression may have multiple operators, not just one. Ignore precedence. For example, 53 + 3 + 5 should give 61

> 12. Complete Key Set: Add the rest of the keys, numeric and operator. The division operator does integer division: 5/3 gives 1. Dividing by zero should throw a run time exception. Alternatively return the minimum integer value.

Note that these are imperfect and incomplete. They were written by an imperfect human, after all. So, if you don't understand anything, ask the one who wrote the story. Even the first story is ambiguous. It talks about a *new* calculator, but the intent was likely about when the calculator was *turned on*. And Story 8 should probably have been split into two stories.

If you make assumptions about the meaning of a story you may be wrong. That isn't devastating as long as your iteration time is short enough that you can correct direction quickly and you have access to the story owner. This is one reason that it is called *Agile Programming*.

Normally the story cards are hand written. They were printed for this exercise simply for distribution to the various pairs in the class. Also, the customer will, in most projects, create new cards as the development progresses, but can only introduce a new story between iterations. Within an iteration the team has a fixed work plan. The professor treated each individual story as an iteration here, but it is usually a set of stories, negotiated in size between developers and customer. Developers also provide an estimate of the work effort for each story, but that isn't explored in this book. Students initially have little basis for an estimate of time required. But recording their time puts them on the path to gaining this skill.

Notes

ad hoc: formed, arranged, or done for a particular purpose only. In programming it means writing explicit tests in IF and SWITCH statements. Contrast with Polymorphism.

Agile Software Development: A family of team-based methodologies that permit and encourage change throughout the development process. For example, XP and Scrum.

Assertion: An executable statement that, if false, will cause the test to fail with a message. More generally, false assertions can cause a program to halt.

Design Pattern: A standard way to solve a common problem.

Eclipse: An integrated development environment that aids the programmer manage the files in an application. It automates many tasks and gives good feedback about errors.

Extreme Programming (XP): A team-based development methodology with about a dozen key practices. Among them are Pair Programming, Test First, and Onsite Customer. The customer gives work to the programmers using Story Cards and a small set of story cards is intended to represent a couple of weeks work for the team: an Iteration. It is Agile.

Flag: A boolean (usually) variable, initially false, that is set to true when some interesting event occurs. The value is later tested in an IF statement to see whether or not the event happened. Multiple-value flags are also possible. In Java, Enumerations are useful as flags, and they can have methods (behavior), so can act like strategies.

Gold Star: A simple, but public, appreciation of a student's good work.

Grade It Again, Sam: A Pedagogical Pattern that suggests students should get a second chance.

Inner Class: A class contained within another. Its methods can see and use the containing-class features. They are often used to build parts of the containing class.

JUnit: A powerful testing framework for Java (Java Unit). It integrates well with development environments such as Eclipse. There are *units* for other languages also.

Null Object: An object that implements an expected interface and is used in place of the null value. It normally implements either empty or default behavior when invoked.

Polymorphism: A way of programming that moves different, but related, behaviors into different objects.

Refactoring: Improving the structure, maintainability, or readability of code without altering its functionality. It can be as simple as changing the name of a variable or as complex as updating an architecture.

Say It Once: A principle of programming that suggests you should not repeat code in a program. Factor the repeated code into a method or an object.

Story: A short description of a single feature of an application written on an index card. An indication that work is needed.

Strategy: An object to which another object delegates part of its responsibility. A flag with behavior.

Test Driven Development (TDD): A technique in which tests are written before the code that is tested. The tests fail, of course, but then the application is updated just enough to make them pass. The watchword is "No Code Without a Failing Test."

The Doctor: No, the Other Doctor.

UML: Unified Modeling Language. A graphical language of design.

For Instructors Only

I'd like to emphasize the advantages of a few of the things developed here.

First, I think that Pair Programming is a big win for you and for your students. Collaboration is one of the things every student needs to learn, no matter what subject is studied. Students can and do help each other learn. This is true even when the perceived abilities of the two students are quite different. When anyone programs, he or she sometimes gets stuck. But two people programming together don't usually get stuck at the same point. You can switch the pairs around over the course of a term to get a sense of individual accomplishment. You can also use Peer Grading to see who is contributing and how. Peer evaluation is needed, in any case, if student team work occurs outside your personal view. But the students need to be able to do the kind of exercise described here face to face. Or shoulder to shoulder, actually. Virtual Pairing is difficult and requires specialized tools. It's not for beginners.

If you use Pair Programming on larger projects, each team should use it within the team, changing partners between stories. A pair takes responsibility for the initial development of a story. They are allowed to modify code of other pairs (*team* ownership of all code). The pair records its time for a story to form the initial basis for skill in estimation. They can only learn how fast they can go through recording their experience. They can write the time on the cards. A personal notebook is also a useful adjunct.

Second, the presentation of programming problems as a collection of stories, rather than as a narrative has many advantages if you are teaching programming primarily and not design. In effect, you do the overall design and let the students focus on lower level things. Also, it helps them to see good designs before needing to produce their own. You can sequence the stories as was done here, or simply group them into a small set of packets of a few stories each, one packet per iteration. But you will need a way to address questions, since the stories aren't complete specifications. I normally use a class-wide mailing list to which everyone is subscribed. Questions from any pair/team go to the list so that everyone can see and benefit from the questions of others. You then only need to answer a question once. Don't be afraid to modify the stories as you go along, especially with more advanced students. Don't be afraid to drop or add stories as a larger project advances. But warn the students in advance that this can happen. An advantage of this is that the students will be less inclined to try to build the application all at once, rather than via piecemeal development.

I like Eclipse a lot. NetBeans works similarly. Since JUnit is such a big part of the methodology, you want to use an IDE that will integrate it well, as these do. In Eclipse, for example, you can use a (right click) pop-up menu to create a new JUnit test, a new class or interface, enter a skeleton for a method first introduced in a test, and many other things. The student mainly types content, not the surrounding headers, etc. Java's "wordiness" becomes less of an issue. And Eclipse supports other languages as well.

Testing First speeds you up. Tests are quick and easy to create, mainly with *copy-paste-update*. The tests keep you on task and focus your work. You aren't nearly as likely to program based on speculation about what you might want in the future. Just make the test pass. Assure you have enough tests for the story. You must also assure that you have a correct understanding of the story, but that is a different issue. It is addressed by different means in XP (Acceptance Tests – not discussed here). But it should be easy to ask the story owner if and when students have any doubts. And, as seen above, the test occasionally points you to the solution.

In this case study, at least, Object-Orientation is not primarily about reusability, encapsulation, and information hiding. It is about being able to create code in a *piecemeal* way from small, understandable, maintainable parts. It is a *craft* technique, not a manufacturing technique. We don't speculate about which classes, hence objects, will be needed. But we purpose-build objects to meet a need. You can, and people do, build applications starting with an incomplete understanding of the final result. After all, things change in most large projects. You just need a few stories to start.

And, most important, note that the students built all of this without a single IF statement. Polymorphic programming is an alternative to ad hoc decision making. My point, however, is not that there is no place for IF statements, but that IF shouldn't be the only technique known by students for making decisions in code. I've seen professional programmers get truly and firmly stuck in their own code in a *single page* of nested decision structures. The mind isn't well designed to keep track of such things. I prefer to teach polymorphism before selection for this reason. The *Polymorphism Étude* is a learning exercise in which a student is tasked with building a program using no IF or SWITCH statements.

The McCabe Cyclomatic Complexity of the code here is 1. So the objects have simple behavior. The complexity is in the interactions.

In order to get the students started with this, I normally do a classroom demonstration in which I take the driver role for a while and let a student take the navigator role. We build a few stories, writing tests and then code. I can demonstrate the features of Eclipse and how they are used to enter the skeletons. Along the way I think out loud about why I'm taking each step. Perhaps I switch roles with my partner. Perhaps I invite someone else to take my seat. Then, I have all the students pair off and try it while I wander around helping as needed. Students come to speed quickly.

While we have only seen polymorphism within a single class, it will also scale to a collection of independent, top-level, classes. In fact, whenever you implement an interface in multiple ways in a program you can substitute one object for another when the behavior needs to change. You will need to pass information in parameters, of course, and find ways to make the substitution of objects as needed. I've found hash maps useful for this, with the objects implementing the behaviors as the map's values and the discriminators as keys. This is powerful when you have a *lot* of different potential behaviors and must *frequently* do selections in a program. You can also add and remove behaviors dynamically by inserting and removing from the map.

The code presented here would be a bit different in other object-oriented languages, such as Python or Ruby. Those two languages are *dynamic,* which implies that there are fewer enforced language rules. Variables, such as fields, don't themselves have type. Only objects do. There is no concept of an enforced *interface*, for example. On the other hand, functions in those languages act like (usually immutable) objects. Therefore a variable can refer directly to a function. So instead of classes to define the strategy objects, we would use *function objects*. The underlying ideas are the same, but the implementation a bit different. The simplicity of the structure of the code is maintained. Note that on pg. 42, Zahid has discussed the current strategy as if it were a function ("...doesn't get executed..."). It is actually an object, but Zahid's view is correct. It acts like a function object, similar to Python or Ruby.

One advantage of Java is that its strong type system helps to enforce programmer intent. The corresponding disadvantage is that it is more verbose and requires the programmer to write things that can be considered redundant. But that, in itself, enables a tool like Eclipse to give more feedback on errors as you type.

It is the *enforced* interface in Java, actually, that makes polymorphism a powerful technique for piecemeal development. If a class implements an interface, it must have every method defined by the interface. It makes it impossible to forget a case when you must repeat a decision structure in a large program. Each case is just the implementation of a method of the existing interface that you defined the first time you visited the situation. Java won't let you quit until you have every method implemented. Python isn't so fussy, so the safeguard isn't as strong. See http://joe.fed.wiki.org for more.

One final thought, and the main point of this book. You shouldn't ignore polymorphism as a skill any more than you should ignore recursion or writing classes and interfaces. It takes a bit to wrap your mind around it, but is a good organizing principle in many programs. Take the Polymorphism Challenge. Practice the Polymorphism Étude. Poetically.

Do good work. Be nice. Stay healthy. Have fun. Peace.

Readings

Beck and Andries: *Extreme Programming Explained: Embrace Change*, 2nd Edition, Addison-Wesley, November 2004

Bergin: *Agile Software: Patterns of Practice*, Joseph Bergin Software Tools, 2012

Bergin: Coding At The Lowest Level, http://csis.pace.edu/~bergin/patterns/codingpatterns.html

Bergin: Polymorphism, http://joe.fed.wiki.org

Bergin: The Polymorphism Étude, http://csis.pace.edu/~bergin/PolymorphismEtude.html

Bergin: XP Patterns of Practice, http://pop.fed.wiki.org

Bergin, Stehlik, Roberts, and Pattis: *Karel J Robot: A Gentle Introduction to the Art of Object-Oriented Programming in Java*, Dream Songs Press, February 2005

Derby and Larsen: *Agile Retrospectives: Making Good Teams Great*, Pragmatic Bookshelf, 2006

Pedagogical Patterns Editorial Board, Joseph Bergin Editor: *Pedagogical Patterns: Advice for Educators*, Joseph Bergin Software Tools, 2012

tutorialspoint: Eclipse Tutorial, http://www.tutorialspoint.com/eclipse

tutorialspoint: Design Patterns in Java Tutorial, http://www.tutorialspoint.com/design_pattern

Various: The Agile Manifesto, http://agilemanifesto.org

Vogel: Unit Testing with JUnit - Tutorial http://www.vogella.com/tutorials/JUnit/article.html

Williams and Kessler: *Pair Programming Illuminated*, Addison-Wesley, July 2002